FRIENDS
OF ACPL

lo3

★ *GREAT SPORTS TEAMS* ★

THE BOSTON

CELTICS

BASKETBALL TEAM

David Pietrusza

D1501353

Enslow Publishers, Inc.
40 Industrial Road   PO Box 38
Box 398   Aldershot
Berkeley Heights, NJ 07922   Hants GU12 6BP
USA   UK

http://www.enslow.com

Library of Congress Cataloging-in-Publication Data

Pietrusza, David, 1949–
    The Boston Celtics basketball team / David Pietrusza.
        p. cm. — (Great sports teams)
    Includes bibliographical references (p.) and index.
    Summary: Discusses the history of the Boston basketball franchise and their
many NBA championships, as well as such key personalities as Bill Russell,
Larry Bird, and Red Auerbach.
    ISBN 0-7660-1747-8 (pbk)
    ISBN 0-7660-1019-8 (library ed.)
    1. Boston Celtics (Basketball team)—History—Juvenile literature. [1. Boston
Celtics (Basketball team)—History. 2. Basketball—History.] I. Title. II. Series.
    GV885.52.B67P54   1998
    796.323′64′0974461—dc21   97-20377
                                                           CIP
                                                            AC

Printed in the United States of America

10 9 8 7 6 5 4 3 2

To Our Readers:
All Internet addresses in this book were active and appropriate when we
went to press. Any comments or suggestions can be sent by e-mail to
Comments@enslow.com or to the address on the back cover.

Illustration Credits: AP/Wide World Photos, pp. 4, 7, 8, 10, 13, 14, 16,
19, 20, 22, 25, 26, 28, 31, 32, 34, 37, 38.

Cover Illustration: AP/Wide World Photos.

CONTENTS

1 A Dynasty Begins 5

2 The Russell Era 11

3 Celtic Greats. 17

4 It Started With Red 23

5 The Big '80s. 29

6 Rebuilding 35

Statistics 40

Chapter Notes. 43

Glossary. 45

Further Reading 46

Index 47

Where to Write
and Internet Sites. 48

*T*ommy Heinsohn of the Celtics jumps for a rebound against Cliff Hagan of the St. Louis Hawks during a 1957 playoff game.

I n the early 1950s the Celtics were just another National Basketball Association (NBA) team— and not always a very good one at that. Unlikely as it seems, Boston had gone its first ten NBA seasons without a championship—or without even making it to the Finals.

That changed in the club's eleventh season (1956–57), when Coach Red Auerbach's Celtics captured the NBA's Eastern Division with a sparkling 44–28 (.611) record. Boston rolled over the Syracuse Nationals in the Division Finals, but ran into unexpected trouble in the NBA Finals against the St. Louis Hawks, who had compiled an anemic 34–38 record in capturing the NBA's Western Division.

An Intense Rivalry

Game 1 went into overtime, with St. Louis eventually winning, 125–123. Games 3 and 6 were decided by just two points each. In St. Louis in Game 3, Auerbach had punched Hawks owner Ben Kerner. Kerner had sworn at Auerbach after Auerbach had complained about the height of the basket. Auerbach had been the coach of the Hawks when they were the Tri-Cities Blackhawks. "I remember Red and Ben rolling around on the floor," recalled St. Louis Hawks Hall of Famer Bob Pettit, "it was just part of the intense rivalry you had between the Celtics and the Hawks."[1] Now on April 13, 1957, it all came down to Game 7.

A sports writer asked Kerner if he wanted Auerbach arrested. "That would be the worst thing," a bleeding Kerner muttered, "I'd rather have him on the bench. We have a better chance to win with him on the [Celtics] bench."[2] Authorities fined Auerbach the then-staggering sum of $300.

The air was electric at the Boston Garden before Game 7. Boston posted an early lead, but St. Louis battled back and led 28–26 as the first quarter ended. The Celtics put it into gear once more, and at one point, led 41–32. Then, six-foot four-inch forward Cliff Hagan registered six points as the second quarter ended. At the half, St. Louis held a narrow 53–51 lead.

A Fantastic Final

By the third quarter the Celtics had outshot St. Louis 73–68. In the fourth quarter they led by a solid eight-point margin. Then St. Louis scored nine unanswered points, taking the lead with less than two minutes to play. The Celtics responded by making three free throws, narrowing their deficit to 101–100. With less

*T*ommy Heinsohn reaches for a loose ball as Bill Russell looks to make sure things are under control.

than a minute to play, Hawks forward Jack Coleman attempted a driving layup that would have put the game out of reach. However, Bill Russell, whose unprecedented defensive play would prove to be the key to establishing the Celtics' winning tradition, provided an amazing block to stop Coleman.

Cousy tied the game with a free throw, and the contest rolled into overtime. Cousy had shot just 2-for-20. His teammate Bill Sharman was only 3-for-20, but two Boston rookies—center Bill Russell, with 19 points and 32 rebounds, and forward Tommy

A Dynasty Begins

*G*liding through the air, Bob Cousy is about to
dish out a no-look pass.

Heinsohn, with 37 points and 23 rebounds—came through in grand fashion. Heinsohn fouled out, but the Celtics still went ahead. Then, Jack Coleman sunk a tough jump shot just before the buzzer sounded, again tying the contest. Now it was double-overtime. Boston inched ahead once again, 125–123, on Jim Loscutoff's two free throws. Still the Hawks kept coming, kept scheming, kept trying.

The Last Shot

With just one second remaining, six-foot seven-inch Hawks player-coach Alex Hannum inserted himself into the game—the first time he had appeared in the Finals. He had a trick play, a desperation move, in mind—one he had developed when he had played with the former Rochester Royals. He launched an amazing length-of-the-court-inbounds pass off the Hawks backboard. It ricocheted—on purpose—to St. Louis frontcourt star Bob Pettit. Pettit attempted a shot. The ball kissed the rim, but fell off as the buzzer sounded. The Boston Celtics were champions of the world.

No one suspected it, but this was only the beginning of the greatest dynasty in sports history.

*B*ill Russell pulls a rebound away from Cliff Hagan (16). Russell led the Celtics to their first NBA Championship in his rookie season.

THE RUSSELL ERA

The Boston Celtics franchise had come into existence in 1946–47 when the NBA had first started and was known as the Basketball Association of America (BAA). At first the Celtics lost games—and lost money. Some thought the team would go out of business. Yet in the early 1950s the Celtics began to get better—good enough to win, but not good enough to reach the top. "With all the talent we've got on this ball club," Coach Red Auerbach fumed in 1956, "if we can just come up with one big man to get us the ball, we'll win everything in sight."[1]

The Big Man

That man turned out to be William Felton "Bill" Russell, who had led the previously undistinguished University of San Francisco Dons to 26 straight wins and the 1955 and 1956 NCAA titles. The Celtics drafted Russell and outbid the barnstorming Harlem Globetrotters for his services. At Boston, Russell joined a talented team that already boasted Bob Cousy and Bill Sharman.

The six-foot nine-and-a-half-inch, 220-pound Russell was a new kind of star. He never once led the Celtics, let alone the NBA, in scoring. Defense and rebounding were the keys to Bill Russell's game. He could block a shot or grab a rebound better than anyone. Over the course of his career he collected 21,620 rebounds, averaging 22.5 per game. He once snared 51 rebounds in a single game. Two other times he collected 49. For twelve straight seasons he had better than 1,000 rebounds each year.

A Most Valuable Player

Five times (1958, 1961–63, 1965) Russell was selected the NBA's Most Valuable Player (MVP); twelve times he was an NBA All-Star. In 1980, the Professional Basketball Writers Association of America voted Russell the Greatest Player in the History of the NBA. From 1956, until his retirement in 1969, Russell led the Celtics to eleven NBA titles—an unprecedented eleven world championships in just thirteen years.

Russell's greatest rivalry was with seven-foot one-inch center Wilt "the Stilt" Chamberlain, who pursued a far different style than Russell's. Chamberlain was as good at putting a ball through a hoop as Russell was at preventing someone from scoring. Once Chamberlain scored 100 points in a single contest; seven times he scored over 70 points in a game. Yet when

Using his quick first step, Sam Jones dribbles past Elgin Baylor of the Los Angeles Lakers.

Chamberlain met Russell head-to-head, the Celtics usually came out on top, posting an 87–60 record.

Bill Russell, however, was not an easy player to like. Sensitive to criticism, he wore a goatee in an era when few athletes (or persons) did. He went out of his way to conserve energy and ostentatiously would walk, rather than run to center court for pre-game ceremonies, and he refused to sign autographs. "I can honestly say," Russell once admitted, "that I have never worked to be liked. I have worked only to be respected. If I am liked, then that is a bonus point of the world we inhabit. If I am disliked, it is the

The Russell Era

*T*ommy Heinsohn of Boston is challenged for a rebound by Dolph Schayes of the Syracuse Nationals. The Nationals' Earl Lloyd (11) looks to get in on the action.

privilege of those who wish to dislike me—as long as it is not based on prejudice."[2]

The Russell-era Celtics were, of course, led by Bill Russell's defensive genius. Yet they were not a one-person show. Guard Bob Cousy passed and dribbled with the best of them. Forwards Sam Jones and Tommy Heinsohn were scoring machines. Guard Frank Ramsey gave the team a dependable "sixth man."

Player-Coach

The last two championships of the Russell Era came in 1968 and 1969. In 1969 Russell (in his third year of coaching the team) was no longer the player he once had been. His knees bothered him so much that he could not even practice, and playing was as much physical wear-and-tear as he could stand. Still, his team captured the NBA East with a 48–34 record, then rolled over Philadelphia and New York before facing the NBA West champion Los Angeles Lakers. The Lakers (who had finished just fourth in their division, but who had stormed to victory in their division playoffs) were confident of victory, and had 5,000 balloons suspended in nets hung from the ceiling of their Forum set to drop in anticipation of a win. The aging Celtics built up a 17-point lead in the fourth quarter of Game 7, but had to struggle to hold on to a two-point margin of victory. The Lakers' balloons stayed where they were. An emotionally exhausted Russell announced his retirement as both a player and a coach.

It would be nineteen years before another NBA team would capture back-to-back titles.

The Russell Era

*D*etermined to reach the basket, Larry Bird drives against Rodney McCray of the Houston Rockets.

CELTIC GREATS

ill Russell was clearly the Celtics' brightest star, but he was hardly alone in Boston's galaxy of talent.

Bob Cousy

Boston's first great star was, of course, Bob Cousy—the "local yokel" Coach Red Auerbach originally didn't want. Blessed with extraordinary peripheral vision, Cousy was noted for his fine passing. If there was a way to find an open man, the "Houdini of the Hardwood" would find it. "He made the blindest passes that were so accurate and perfectly timed they left fans gasping," noted author Martin Taragano. "Many times his teammates and coaches were awestruck as well."[1] He paced the NBA in assists eight times and was a part of six Boston championships. When the club captured its first title, the six-foot one-inch Cousy was named the NBA's MVP.

Larry Bird

Hustling, confident, six-foot nine-inch forward Larry Bird was another great passer. "While no one could make all the passes he could," marveled *Boston Globe* columnist Bob Ryan, "by playing with him a man began to think in terms of passing. When all five men on the court are committed to that end, wonderful things can happen."[2] Some of the wonderful things that Bird accomplished included the 1980 NBA Rookie of the Year, three consecutive (1984–86) NBA MVP awards (only Bill Russell and Wilt Chamberlain had previously accomplished that feat), three Celtics NBA titles (1981, 1984, and 1986), and ten Atlantic Division crowns. In return, Celtics fans took Bird into their hearts. "Watching Larry Bird play became a privilege," sportswriters Bob Ryan and Terry Pluto noted. "Dazed basketball aficionados wandered around asking themselves, 'What wonderful thing did I ever do to deserve *this*?'"[3]

John Havlicek

The six-foot five-inch John Havlicek is the all-time Celtics scoring leader, both career-wise, with 26,395 points, and for one season (1970–71), with 2,338 points. A thirteen-time all-star, Havlicek was always in motion. "My game has always been to go as hard as I can, as long as I can."[4] His most famous play came in the seventh game of the 1964–65 Eastern Division Finals. With Boston leading Philadelphia 110–109 and just five seconds left, the 76ers' Johnny Kerr made an inbounds pass to Chet Walker. If Walker succeeded

*J*ohn Havlicek looks to grab the rebound before the Lakers' Wilt Chamberlain is able to get to it. Havlicek has scored more points than any other Celtic.

with his shot it was all over for the Celtics. Instead, Havlicek intercepted the ball, deflecting it to teammate Sam Jones. Celtics announcer Johnny Most screamed, "Havlicek stole the ball!" over and over again. Boston's championship had been saved.

Sam Jones

Guard/forward Sam Jones was another Celtics great. Jones played on ten NBA Championship teams during his twelve-year Celtics career. Some said Jones

Kevin McHale reaches around Dell Curry of the Utah Jazz in order to get an open shot.

had the best bank shot of all time. His career one-game high was an impressive 51 points.

Robert Parish

Robert Parish—"The Chief"—played NBA ball into his forties. On April 6, 1996, the seven-foot center (then with the Charlotte Hornets) played in his 1,561st game and passed the great Kareem Abdul-Jabbar as the all-time leader in NBA games played. He ended the NBA season—his record 21st—with 1,568 games played. Parish ranks in the top ten in NBA history in rebounding, blocked shots, and minutes played. "I never thought I'd be playing this long—period," he admits.[5] Parish, who performed on the 1981, 1984, and 1986 NBA championship squads, is Boston's all-time leader with 1,703 blocked shots. Parish retired following the 1996–97 season.

Kevin McHale

Kevin McHale is usually remembered as the best "sixth man" of all time. The six-foot ten-inch McHale was unusually quick and dexterous for a man his size—and that paid off as he, Larry Bird, and Robert Parish formed the "Big Three," perhaps the most powerful frontcourt of all time. "Throwing the ball to Kevin McHale," wrote Bob Ryan and Terry Pluto in 1987, "has become the surest way any team has to get two points at any given moment in the NBA."[6]

Not surprisingly, in 1996 when the NBA—on its 50th anniversary—named its 50 Greatest Players, Bird, Cousy, Havlicek, Sam Jones, McHale, Parish, and Russell all made the list.

Possibly the greatest coach in NBA history, Red Auerbach has won more championships than anyone else. Auerbach is shown here holding his trademark cigar.

IT STARTED WITH RED

The Celtics were one of the most successful franchises in all of professional sports. And clearly the Celtics' most famous and influential coach was the controversial Red Auerbach, noted for lighting up a victory cigar when he thought his team had the game wrapped up.

Red Auerbach

Auerbach joined the Celtics for the 1950–51 season, but did not produce a champion—or even reach the Finals—until 1956–57. His first move with the team was his worst, refusing to draft Holy Cross guard Bob Cousy and disdainfully dismissing Cousy as "a local yokel."[1]

Luckily for Auerbach—and the Celtics—Cousy ended up with Boston anyway, after the Chicago Stags folded and Boston owner Walter Brown won the rights to Cousy by pulling his name out of a hat.

Cousy made the team respectable; Bill Russell made it a champion; but the constant in the Celtics' equation was Red Auerbach. Intense strategizing was not a key to the Auerbach success formula. He had a set number of straightforward plays that he ran over and over again. "Most people think Red was a basketball genius," said Tommy Heinsohn, "an X and O guy, but he wasn't. His strength was in management, being in control."[2]

Auerbach's most famous habit—aside from winning championships—was lighting up his famous "victory cigar." "When the league was picking on me, I tried to think of something that would aggravate the higher-ups," he once revealed. "I wasn't having much luck until one day I lighted up a cigar during the game. Afterward I got a little note saying, 'It doesn't look good for you to be smoking cigars on the bench.' I haven't been without one since."[3]

Nine times Auerbach won NBA titles, eleven times he coached NBA All-Star teams (and won seven times). Boasting an NBA regular-season coaching record of 938–479 (1,037–548, including postseason play), Auerbach retired in 1966 to become Celtics general manager (GM). In 1984 he moved upstairs again, becoming Celtics president. In 1980 the Basketball Writers Association named him the "Greatest Coach in the History of the NBA."

Bill Russell

Auerbach's most momentous decision as GM involved who his successor as coach would be. In

*A*fter Red Auerbach stepped away from the bench, Bill Russell coached the Celtics for three years. Russell led his team to the NBA title in two of those seasons.

choosing Bill Russell, Auerbach hired the first African-American head coach or manager in any major American team sport. It was not the first time the Celtics had opened the door to African-American talent. In 1950 Walter Brown had become the first NBA owner to draft an African-American player, six-foot five-inch Duquesne forward Chuck Cooper. "I

A former Celtics player, K. C. Jones became the team's head coach in 1983. He retired in 1988 after winning two NBA Championships with the team, in 1984 and 1986.

don't give a damn if he's striped or polka dot or plaid," Brown supposedly said when another owner tried to talk him out of it. "Boston takes Charles Cooper of Duquesne."[4]

Auerbach paid Russell a salary of $100,001—one dollar more than Russell's archrival Wilt Chamberlain was earning in Philadelphia. After being eliminated in the second round of the 1966–67 season, Russell proved himself by continuing the team's winning tradition and capturing NBA titles in 1967–68 and 1968–69.

Tommy Heinsohn

Russell went out on top, retiring after 1969. He was succeeded by another distinguished Celtic alumni, Tommy Heinsohn. Heinsohn did not fare as well, but still won two NBA titles in his nine seasons on the Boston Garden bench. In 1973 he was named NBA Coach of the Year—the only man to be named both NBA Rookie of the Year and Coach of the Year.

K. C. Jones

Another former Celtics star, K. C. Jones, took over the reins in 1983–84 and promptly led the team to its fifteenth championship, winning again in 1985–86. Jones, a teammate of Russell at the University of San Francisco, played on eight Celtics NBA championship teams. He owns the fourth-highest won-lost percentage of any NBA coach (.661). During the 1996–97 season he served as an assistant to then-Celtics coach M. L. Carr.

*W*ith fierce determination, Robert Parish hauls down a rebound. The Celtics' fortunes began to improve after Parish was acquired in a trade prior to the 1980–81 season.

THE BIG '80s

The Celtics returned to the top of the basketball heap in the early 1980s, featuring such franchise standouts as Larry Bird, forward/center Kevin McHale (winner of two Sixth Man Awards), guards Danny Ainge and Dennis Johnson, and center Robert Parish.

1981

Before the start of the 1980–81 season, Red Auerbach pulled off a trade that would once again revitalize his team. He obtained veteran center Robert Parish from Golden State and put himself in a position to take McHale as the number three pick overall in the 1980 NBA draft. These talented newcomers joined with Larry Bird and forward Cedric Maxwell to bring Coach Bill Fitch and the Celtics the team's first championship since 1975–76. In conquering Houston in that season's Finals, Bird made one play that still has people talking. From eighteen feet out he launched a shot, but as soon as he released it he knew it would miss. He raced in to grab the rebound. Bird snagged the rebound about twelve feet away from the basket. In mid-air he switched the ball to his left hand and launched another shot. Swish. "It was the best shot I've ever seen a player make," Red Auerbach claimed.[1]

1984

In 1983–84 the Celtics had a new coach, K. C. Jones—and another championship. That year Bird finally faced the NBA's other great superstar, the Lakers' Magic Johnson, in the Finals. The Celtics had their work cut out for them. They lost Game 1 and were on the verge of losing Game 2 when Boston's Gerald Henderson intercepted Lakers forward James Worthy's crosscourt pass and tied the game with an easy layup. Boston went on to win 124–121 in overtime. The Celtics lost Game 3, but Game 4 was another overtime tussle captured by Boston. "To be honest, they should have swept," Bird admitted.[2] The Finals went all the way, with Boston taking Game 7 111–102 before what was then the largest television audience in the history of the NBA.

1986

The Celtics and Lakers tangled again in the 1984–85 Finals. This time L.A. won in six. Yet the Celtics came storming back in 1985–86, having traded Cedric Maxwell to the Los Angeles Clippers for veteran

The Boston Celtics Basketball Team

*V*eteran center Bill Walton provided some much needed bench strength during the 1986 season.

*C*eltics guard Dennis Johnson wipes the blood from his face after being involved in a fight with one of the Houston players during the 1986 NBA Finals.

center Bill Walton. As Bird earned his third straight NBA MVP Award, the Celtics captured the Atlantic Conference. At home in the Boston Garden they were an incredible 40–1.

In the postseason, the Celtics stormed past Chicago, Atlanta, and Milwaukee on their way to the

The Boston Celtics Basketball Team

Finals. There they faced seven-foot, 250-pound Hakeem Olajuwon and the Houston Rockets, coached by former Celtics coach Bill Fitch. The Celtics took the first two games at home, then traveled to Houston. They expected they would not have to return home, but the Rockets surprised them by taking two out of three in Houston. Adding insult to injury, in Game 5 the Rockets' seven-foot four-inch center Ralph Sampson fought with six-foot one-inch guard Jerry Sichting.

Boston came home angry and determined the Finals would not go to seven games. In Game 6 they steamrolled Houston, 114–97. "I thought it was our best team," said Larry Bird. "We had a great team, and it seemed like everybody did what they had to do to make us a great team. It was a fun year."[3] Boston posted a total of 82 regular season and playoff victories that year, the highest in the history of the NBA up to that time.

The End of an Era

In 1986–87, for the third straight season, Boston posted the NBA's best regular season record—even though Walton and former all-star forward Scott Wedman suffered through injury-plagued seasons. In the playoffs, Boston moved past Chicago, Milwaukee, and Detroit to reach the Finals, once again facing the Lakers. Los Angeles, however, took its fourth NBA title of the 1980s, and Boston was beginning a slow slide from greatness.

*S*ince their last championship in 1986, the
Celtics team has been victimized by several
misfortunes. The death of star guard Reggie
Lewis in 1993 is one example.

6

REBUILDING

A decade of frustration—and tragedy—began for the Celtics in 1984. That year, Boston traded guard Gerald Henderson to the Seattle SuperSonics for a 1986 first-round draft pick. They used that pick in 1986 to select six-foot eight-inch University of Maryland standout Len Bias. He was a can't-miss star, and Reebok immediately signed him to a million-dollar sneaker contract. Two days later, the talented Bias died of cocaine intoxication.

A Slow Decline

Boston continued to win in the regular season, but even with Bird, McHale, and the pugnacious guard Danny Ainge, after 1986–87 the team no longer had the talent to advance to the Finals. Draft choices no longer worked out. Old faces were disappearing. Auerbach traded Ainge to Portland. In 1992 Bird, just thirty-five but bothered by a bad back, retired.

McHale followed him in 1993. That same year the team even lost the long-time voice of the Celtics, Johnny Most, who died at age sixty-nine.

The Celtics hopes rested on popular team captain Reggie Lewis. Yet during the 1993 postseason, the six-foot seven-inch Lewis collapsed during a game against the Charlotte Hornets. He was diagnosed with an irregular heartbeat, but continued to play. During a private workout on July 27, 1993, the twenty-seven-year-old Lewis suffered complete cardiac arrest and died almost immediately.

Losing Seasons

The 1993–94 Celtics finished 32–50 (their first losing season since 1978–79) and a new—and disappointing—Celtic era began. Losing seasons followed in 1994–95 and in 1995–96. The 1995–96 season saw important changes, however. Former Celtics small forward M. L. Carr became Boston's head coach—the third African American (after Russell and K. C. Jones) to guide the club.

Boston also boasted a beautiful new facility to call their home. In September 1995, the $180 million FleetCenter replaced the badly-aging Boston Garden. The Garden, with its fabled parquet floor, possessed a lot of history but was sadly outdated. With 18,600 seats the FleetCenter has 3,710 more seats than the arena it replaced. The FleetCenter brought Celtics basketball into the modern age—featuring air conditioning and unobstructed views, two items the Garden lacked.

In 1996–97, rookie Antoine Walker provided a bright spot in an otherwise dismal season. Walker figures to be a large piece of the puzzle as the Celtics look to turn things around.

Help Begins to Arrive

The key Celtics rookie for 1996–97 was six-foot nine-inch, 225-pound Antoine Walker. Walker, an early entry candidate in the 1996 NBA Draft, helped lead the Wildcats of Kentucky to the NCAA Championship, leading them in rebounding (8.4 per game) and minutes played (27).

Walker joined a Celtics team that boasted no Russells or Birds. Key Celtics were Croatian-born power forward Dino Radja, and five-foot eleven-inch

Rebuilding

*F*ollowing the 1996–97 season, the Boston Celtics hired Rick Pitino to be their new head coach. Pitino led the Kentucky Wildcats to the 1996 NCAA Championship.

guard Dana Barros. Barros holds the NBA record with 89 straight games of making a three-point field goal, breaking Michael Adams's mark of 79 straight.

M. L. Carr, who resigned as coach after the 1996–97 season, had been particularly insistent on building an all-for-one attitude on his often out-gunned team. "You spend enough time together and it's not just your teammate out there, it's your friend," Carr said. "These guys are getting there. They really care about each other."[1]

In 1996–97 the Celtics finished the season at 15–67, last place in the Atlantic Division. Walker, one of the few bright spots, led the team in scoring, averaging 17.5 points per game. Celtics' management was disappointed with the oft-injured Radja and released him after the season.

A New Beginning

During the off-season, the Celtics' front office announced that Rick Pitino had been hired to coach the team. Pitino is most famous for leading the Kentucky Wildcats to the 1996 NCAA Championship. Pitino hopes to turn around the struggling team by adding younger, more talented players.

STATISTICS

Team Record
The Celtics History

YEARS	LOCATION	W	L	PCT	CHAMPIONSHIPS
1946–47 to 1949–50	Boston	89	147	.377	None
1950–51 to 1959–60	Boston	445	268	.624	1957, 1959, 1960
1960–61 to 1969–70	Boston	546	260	.677	1961, 1962, 1963, 1964, 1965, 1966, 1968, 1969
1970–71 to 1979–80	Boston	504	316	.615	1974, 1976
1980–81 to 1989–90	Boston	583	237	.711	1981, 1984, 1986
1990–91 to 1999–00	Boston	360	428	.457	None

W=Wins   L=Losses   PCT=Winning Percentage

The Celtics Today

SEASON	SEASON RECORD	PLAYOFF RECORD	COACH	DIVISION FINISH
1990–91	56–26	5–6	Chris Ford	1st
1991–92	51–31	6–4	Chris Ford	1st
1992–93	48–34	1–3	Chris Ford	2nd
1993–94	32–50	—	Chris Ford	5th
1994–95	35–47	1–3	Chris Ford	3rd
1995–96	33–49	—	M. L. Carr	5th
1996–97	15–67	—	M. L. Carr	7th
1997–98	36–46	—	Rick Pitino	6th
1998–99	19–31	—	Rick Pitino	5th
1999–00	35–47	—	Rick Pitino	5th

The Boston Celtics Basketball Team

Total History

SEASON RECORD	PLAYOFF RECORD	NBA CHAMPIONSHIPS
2,527–1,656	272–189	16

Coaching Record

COACH	YEARS COACHED	RECORD	CHAMPIONSHIPS
John Russell	1946–48	42–66	None
Alvin Julian	1948–50	47–81	None
Red Auerbach	1950–66	795–397	Division Champions, 1958 NBA Champions, 1957, 1959–66
Bill Russell	1966–69	162–83	NBA Champions, 1968, 1969
Tommy Heinsohn	1969–77	427–263	Division Champions, 1972–73, 1975 NBA Champions, 1974, 1976
Tom Sanders	1977–78	23–39	None
Dave Cowens	1978–79	27–41	None
Bill Fitch	1979–83	242–86	Division Champions, 1980, 1982 NBA Champions, 1981
K. C. Jones	1983–88	308–102	Division Champions, 1985, 1987–88 NBA Champions, 1984, 1986
Jimmy Rodgers	1988–90	94–70	None
Chris Ford	1990–95	222–188	Division Champions, 1991–92
M. L. Carr	1995–97	48–116	None
Rick Pitino	1997–00	90–124	None

Ten Great Celtics

				CAREER STATISTICS					
PLAYER	**SEA**	**YRS**	**G**	**REB**	**AST**	**BLK**	**STL**	**PTS**	**AVG**
Larry Bird	1979–92	13	897	8,974	5,695	755	1,556	21,791	24.3
Bob Cousy	1950–63	14	924	4,786	6,955	*	*	16,960	18.4
John Havlicek	1962–78	16	1,270	8,007	6,114	117*	476*	26,395	20.8
Tommy Heinsohn	1956–65	9	654	5,749	1,318	*	*	12,194	18.6
Sam Jones	1957–69	12	871	4,305	2,209	*	*	15,411	17.7
Reggie Lewis	1987–93	6	450	1,938	1,153	417	569	7,902	17.6
Kevin McHale	1980–93	13	971	7,122	1,670	1,690	344	17,335	17.9
Robert Parish	1980–94	21	1,611	14,715	2,180	2,357	1,219	23,334	14.5
Bill Russell	1956–69	13	963	21,620	4,100	*	*	14,522	15.1
Antoine Walker	1996–00	4	288	2,588	970	173	427	5,739	19.9

* Statistics are incomplete for some players in some categories. The NBA did not keep statistics on rebounds until 1950–51 and on steals and blocked shots until 1973–74.

SEA=Seasons with Celtics
YRS=Years in the NBA
G=Games
REB=Rebounds
AST=Assists

BLK=Blocks
STL=Steals
PTS=Total Points
AVG=Scoring Average

The Boston Celtics Basketball Team

CHAPTER NOTES

Chapter 1

1. Dan Shaughnessy, *Seeing Red: The Red Auerbach Story* (Holbrook, Mass.: Adams Publishing, 1994), p. 126.

2. Ibid., p. 127.

Chapter 2

1. Dan Shaughnessy, *Ever Green: The Boston Celtics: A History in the Words of Their Players, Coaches, Fans & Foes, From 1946 to the Present* (New York: St. Martin's Press, 1990), p. 71.

2. Nelson George, *Elevating the Game: Black Men and Basketball* (New York: HarperCollins, 1992), p. 106.

Chapter 3

1. Martin Taragano, *Basketball Biographies* (Jefferson, N.C.: McFarland & Co., 1991), p. 62.

2. Alex Sachare, ed., *The Official NBA Basketball Encyclopedia*, 2nd ed. (New York: Villard Books, 1994), p. 82.

3. Bob Ryan and Terry Pluto, *Forty-Eight Minutes: A Night in the Life of the NBA* (New York: Collier, 1987), p. 79.

4. Greg Garber, *Hoops! Highlights, History, and Stars* (New York: Friedman/Fairfax, 1994), p. 82.

5. David DuPree, "Celtics in Transition: Boston Looks for Identity Without Bird," *USA Today*, December 1, 1992, p. 1C.

6. Ryan and Pluto, p. 135.

Chapter 4

1. Dan Shaughnessy, *Ever Green: The Boston Celtics: A History in the Words of Their Players, Coaches, Fans & Foes, From 1946 to the Present* (New York: St. Martin's Press, 1990), p. 61.

2. Harvey Araton and Filip Bondy, *The Selling of the Green: The Financial Rise and Moral Decline of the Boston Celtics* (New York: HarperCollins, 1992), p. 42.

3. Dan Shaughnessy, *Seeing Red: The Red Auerbach Story* (Holbrook, Mass.: Adams Publishing, 1994), pp. 1–2.

4. Araton and Bondy, p. 51.

Chapter 5

1. Alex Sachare, ed., *The Official NBA Basketball Encyclopedia*, 2nd ed. (New York: Villard Books, 1994), p. 138.

2. Ibid., p. 142.

3. Dan Shaughnessy, *Ever Green: The Boston Celtics: A History in the Words of Their Players, Coaches, Fans & Foes, From 1946 to the Present* (New York: St. Martin's Press, 1990), p. 211.

Chapter 6

1. Michael Holley, "The Good, the Bad and the Ugly: They'll Lose a Lot, But These Celtics are Likable Bunch," *Boston Globe*, November 1, 1996, p. C8.

GLOSSARY

bank shot—A basket made by shooting the ball off the backboard and then into the net.

dribbling—Moving the ball down the court by repeatedly bouncing it.

foul—Illegal physical contact against an opposing player. The ball may then be given to the fouled player's team and/or a free throw (or foul shot) may be awarded.

jump shot—A shot taken after a player has jumped straight up in the air.

period—Each NBA game is divided into four twelve-minute periods—also known as quarters.

overtime—The additional period or periods called for if a game is tied at the end of regulation play. Regulation periods are twelve minutes each; overtime periods are five minutes.

NCAA—The National Collegiate Athletic Association. Since 1939 it has hosted a tournament to determine the national champion college basketball team.

rebound—Grabbing the ball off the backboard after a missed shot. An offensive rebound is taken off the team's own basket or backboard; a defensive rebound is taken off the opposing team's basket or backboard.

swish—A shot that goes through the basket without hitting the backboard or the rim.

timeout—A ninety-second halt in play. During a timeout the clock is stopped.

FURTHER READING

Bjarkman, Peter C. *The Encyclopedia of Pro Basketball: Team Histories.* New York: Carol & Graf, 1994.

George, Nelson. *Elevating the Game: Black Men and Basketball.* New York: HarperCollins, 1992.

Hollander, Zander, ed. *The Complete Handbook of Pro Basketball: 1996 Edition.* New York: Signet, 1995.

Kavanagh, Jack. *Sports Great Larry Bird.* Springfield, N.J.: Enslow Publishers, Inc., 1992.

Knapp, Ron. *Top 10 Basketball Centers.* Springfield, N.J.: Enslow Publishers, Inc., 1994.

Rappoport, Ken. *Top 10 Basketball Legends.* Springfield, N.J.: Enslow Publishers, Inc., 1995.

Sachare, Alex, ed. *The Official NBA Basketball Encyclopedia,* 2nd ed. New York: Villard Books, 1994.

Savage, Jeff. *Top 10 Basketball Point Guards.* Springfield, N.J.: Enslow Publishers, Inc., 1997.

Shaughnessy, Dan. *Ever Green: The Boston Celtics: A History in the Words of Their Players, Coaches, Fans & Foes, From 1946 to the Present.* New York: St. Martin's Press, 1990.

———. *Seeing Red: The Red Auerbach Story.* Holbrook, Mass.: Adams Publishing, 1994.

Taragano, Martin. *Basketball Biographies.* Jefferson, N.C.: McFarland & Co., 1991.

INDEX

A

Abdul-Jabbar, Kareem, 21
Adams, Michael, 39
Ainge, Danny, 29, 35
Atlanta Hawks, 32
Auerbach, Arnold "Red", 5–6,
    11, 17, 23–25, 29, 30, 35

B

Barros, Dana, 39
Basketball Association of
    America (BAA), 11
Bias, Len, 35
Billups, Chauncey, 39
Bird, Larry, 18, 21, 29–30, 33, 35,
    37
Boston Garden, 6, 27, 32, 36
Boston Globe, 18
Brown, Walter, 23, 25, 27

C

Carr, M. L., 27, 36, 39
Chamberlain, Wilt, 12–13, 27
Charlotte Hornets, 21, 36
Chicago Bulls, 32–33
Chicago Stags, 23
Coleman, Jack, 7, 9
College of the Holy Cross, 23
Cooper, Chuck, 25, 27
Cousy, Bob, 7, 12, 15, 17, 21, 23

D

Detroit Pistons, 33
Duquesne University, 25, 27

E

Edney, Tyus, 39

F

Fitch, Bill, 29, 33
FleetCenter, 36

G

Golden State Warriors, 29

H

Hagan, Cliff, 6
Hannum, Alex, 9
Harlem Globetrotters, 12
Havlicek, John, 18–19
Heinsohn, Tommy, 7, 9, 15, 24
Henderson, Gerald, 30, 35
Houston Rockets, 29, 33

J

Johnson, Dennis, 29
Johnson, Magic, 30
Jones, K. C., 27, 30, 36
Jones, Sam, 15, 19, 21

K

Kentucky Wildcats, 37, 39
Kerner, Ben, 6
Kerr, Johnny, 18
Knight, Travis, 39

L

Lewis, Reggie, 36
Los Angeles Clippers, 30
Los Angeles Lakers, 15, 30, 33
Loscutoff, Jim, 9

M

Maxwell, Cedric, 29, 30
McCray, Rodney, 16
McHale, Kevin, 21, 29, 35, 36
Mercer, Ron, 39
Milwaukee Bucks, 32–33
Most, Johnny, 19, 36

N

NBA Playoffs (1957), 5–9
NBA Playoffs (1965), 18–19
NBA Playoffs (1969), 15

NBA Playoffs (1976), 29
NBA Playoffs (1981), 29–30
NBA Playoffs (1984), 30
NBA Playoffs (1986), 32–33
NCAA, 11, 37, 39
New York Knicks, 15

O
Olajuwon, Hakeem, 33

P
Parish, Robert, 21, 29
Pettit, Bob, 6, 9
Philadelphia 76ers, 15, 18, 27
Pitino, Rick, 39
Pluto, Terry, 18, 21
Portland Trailblazers, 35
Professional Basketball Writers
    Association of America, 12, 24

R
Radja, Dino, 37, 39
Ramsey, Frank, 15
Reebok, 35
Rochester Royals, 9

Russell, Bill, 7, 11–13, 15, 17, 21,
    24–25, 27, 36, 37
Ryan, Bob, 18, 21

S
St. Louis Hawks, 5–9
Sampson, Ralph, 33
Seattle SuperSonics, 35
Sharman, Bill, 7, 12
Sichting, Jerry, 33
Syracuse Nationals, 5

T
Taragano, Martin, 17
Tri-Cities Blackhawks, 6

U
University of San Francisco, 11,
    27

W
Walker, Antoine, 37, 39
Walker, Chet, 18
Wallace, Chris, 39
Walton, Bill, 32, 33
Worthy, James, 30

WHERE TO WRITE AND INTERNET SITES

Celtics NBA Web Site
http://www.nba.com/celtics/

Bob Cousy Basketball Hall of Fame
http://www.hoophall.com/
enshrinees/bio.cfm?name=BobCousy

Larry Bird NBA Player File
http://www.nba.com/history/bird_bio.html

Robert Parish NBA Player File
http://www.nba.com/history/parish_bio.html

Kevin McHale NBA Player File
http://www.nba.com/history/mchale_bio.html

ESPN Clubhouse
http://espn.go.com/nba/clubhouses/bos.html

Boston Celtics
151 Merrimac St.
4th Floor
Boston, MA 02114

The Boston Celtics Basketball Team